Foraging

Wesleyan Poetry

Foraging

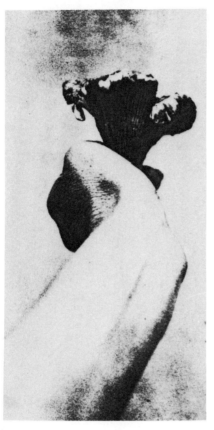

David Young

Wesleyan University Press
Middletown, Connecticut

Some of the poems in this book appeared originally in these
magazines and journals: "Two Trips to Ireland," *Indiana
Review*; "Suite for Jean Follain," *Iowa Review*; "The Self: A
Sonnet Sequence," *Missouri Review*; "October Couplets,"
Ohio Journal; "Elegy in the Form of an Invitation," *Plough-
shares*; "Mesa Verde," *Quarry West*. "In My Own Back
Yard" appeared originally in *The New Yorker*.

This book is supported by a grant from the National
Endowment for the Arts.

Distributed by Harper & Row Publishers, Keystone Indus-
trial Park, Scranton, Pennsylvania 18512.

Library of Congress Cataloging in Publication Data
Young, David P.
    Foraging.
    (Wesleyan poetry)
    I. Title. II. Series.
PS3575.078F6   1986   811'.54   85-5133
ISBN 0-8195-5142-2 (alk. paper)
ISBN 0-8195-6142-8 (pbk.: alk. paper)

Manufactured in the United States of America

First Edition

Wesleyan Poetry

But nature is a stranger yet;
The ones that cite her most
Have never passed her haunted house,
Nor simplified her ghost.

To pity those that know her not
Is helped by the regret
That those who know her, know her less
The nearer her they get.

EMILY DICKINSON

Contents

1

In My Own Back Yard 3
A Ghost, to One Alive 6
Two Trips to Ireland 7
Mesa Verde 10

2

October Couplets 17
Bashō 20
Six Ghosts 24
The Self: A Sonnet Sequence 26

3

Hunting for Mushrooms in Orange County 35
Suite for Jean Follain 37
Elegy in the Form of an Invitation 39
Vermont Summer: Three Snapshots, One Letter 41
Bonuses 44
Three Walks 46

Notes and Dedications 49

In My Own Back Yard

1

July, I'm dozing in sun on the deck,
one thrush is singing among the high trees,
and Li Po walks by, chanting a poem!
He is drunk, he smells unwashed
I can see tiny lice in his hair
and right through him
a brown leaf in the yard
flips over flips
again lies still
all this time
no wind.

2

From behind November glass I watch the wind
truck all its winter furnishings
item by item into my yard.
In a dusty raincoat my neighbor
throws a tennis ball, over and over,
to exercise his police dog.

Sometimes I feel like one of the world's bad
    headaches,
sometimes I think I get no closer
to what I have wanted to mean
than the gumshoe calling
"Testing"
up to the bugged ceiling . . .

You can try to put words to a mood
or tell yourself to ignore it,
but what kind of message is coming

from the chickadee, dapper
in his black mask and skullcap,
grooming himself on the big pine's branch-tip?

His music is small and monotonous,
but it's his own.

3
I am turning pages in lamplight.
Outside, above blue snow, in February dusk,
in the double world of glass,
more pages flip, like wings—
this merging of me and the world
done with mirrors and windows.

4
Hunting for duck eggs at the end of March
I watch three mallards and a speckled female make
a tight flotilla on the swollen creek.

The dog barks at her counterpart
on the other bank. Nothing is green
the way these mallards' heads are green.

Empty-handed, I turn back to the house.
Small waterlights
play on the underbranches of the ash. High up
the sycamore lifts its light-peeled limbs
against a turning sky.

5

Late May. Summer coming on again. I think
Li Po may not be back. Worried about
the world's end, as, I realize
I have been most of my life,
I take my work outside
and sit on the deck, distracted.
It was a day like this, I think,
in Hiroshima.
Distracted.
There must be something in the pine cones
that the chickadees—there's another one.
What's this that's snowing down? Husks, pollen,
freckle-sized petals from our wild cherry trees!

We sneeze and plant tomatoes. Ultimatums. The
  world
comes close and goes away
in rhythms that our years
help us begin to understand.

We haven't long to live.
And the world? Surely the world . . .
A deep breath. Sunshine.
Mosquitoes, bird calls, petal-hail.

A Ghost, to One Alive

There you sit, in the midst of your heart's rich tick,
your breath coming and going,
a lax and happy piston;

your eyes blink, your tongue slicks your lips,
your brain hums, gobbling oxygen.
Oh hot, unconscious life . . .

I know I am hard to imagine—
a smoke-bag, a spindle of mist, fume of an old
    fear-pot—
but you are just the opposite:

you ruin this sweet hush, two times too real,
and I find I have to drift back
from your clicks, wheezes and smells,

your mask of hope over a hopeless gape,
one eye on the wagging clock, muffled
amazement, bundle of hungers, oven stuffed with
    yourself!

If you knew a bit more you might envy me,
moon-scalded as I am,
voodoo-hooded and vague as cheesecloth,

a simulacrum of solid old you,
the last billow from a cold, closed furnace,
a dimple, at best, in existence,

the bird call without the bird.

Two Trips to Ireland

1

Well-eye, gazing at daytime stars,
rain-speckle, patches of blooming mists,
a hillside white with water-spill,
a shower blowing inland at the coast . . .

All this water must *mean* something!

2

Long deserted glens in the Wicklow Hills
and an axe, buried in a tree so long
only the tip of the handle shows.

3

The small hotel in Gort, ale and roast lamb,
the midday drowse. Who breathed this air?
Who climbed these stairs? Time floats,
one face of a diamond, scraps of paper in the street.

4

From these ruined beehive huts
on the bright slope you can see
half the Dingle and
the distant winking sea.

Monks, who had to be
gone in the head.
Where's their god now?
Look closer at the cross-eyed pup
that followed you up this slant pasture,
the heifer that kneels, gazing out
on miles of sun and rain-washed air.

5

And the wind, a mind that's never still,
with its black thoughts, the rooks at Cashel,
its white thoughts, the sea gulls at New Grange,
all this tossing and cawing among great ruins.

6

Lissadell: cracks, tatters, stains.
An old lady in gumboots
shepherds a handful of tourists;
from an upstairs window
you strain to see the past,
horses like swans, peacocks on gravel,
cloudburst at four and dress for dinner . . .

Night fog. Ghosts in the garden,
ghosts on the stair,
ghost of an old fiddler, air threading the air.

7

On a back road by a tower
a movie crew, Arthurians lunching.
Why not? Time-levels mix like bones
in pasture-battlefield, bog-shrine.
Iseult still boils spuds for the pig
and Tristan, cutting turf, turns up
a Roman coin or a telephone cable.
That Viking ship below the Moher Cliffs
is a film prop or another fold
in the wrinkled suit of time.

8

The river Fergus
runs like a wild clock
by the tumbledown house we rent
on a cold lake in County Clare.
Near the ruins of the mill
I catch an eel and, feeling a fool,
I let him go.
A local rod and tackle man
who comes and goes like a ghost in the dusk
says I could have kept him 'for a pie,'
then hints at what I ought to know:
the trout are far too smart
to let themselves be caught
by a man so trapped in time.

Mesa Verde

1

Drive up with me.

Show the way, magpie, across the invisible bridge.

Old ghosts, be near,
but not too near.

September, early morning, not a trace of haze.
Rabbit brush glows like sulphur
and the mesa dozes in sunlight.
The corner-eye specter on the trail
is a rock or a pinyon stump
or a tourist aiming a camera.
Sun-shimmer and squint. The gorges
lie silent and waterless
like dreams of river valleys
that rivers never made.

Climb into me, Anasazi,
take my tongue and language,
tell how you came to farm the corn,
hoarding the snow-melt, learned
to be weavers, potters, masons
in the huge American daylight,
gathering pine nuts, hunting mule deer,
crushed juniper berries with water,
mixed them in cornmeal for our thick blue bread
—what was our word for bread?—
and praised the gods, hunched in our smoky kivas,
singing over the soul-hole
the mystery of our birth

when first a man crawled out
from warm dark to open air.

We farmed till the droughts got worse,
the corn and squash and beans
shriveled and died, the game thinned out,
and we moved down to live
in the scoops and pockets of cliffs
where water seeped and food could be hoarded,
two hundred feet below the dizzy rim,
nine hundred feet above the canyon floor
perching like squirrels and jays
because the gods decided
(what were the names of the gods?)
that life had been too easy,
that snows should stop and water shrink
and we too nest against the canyon walls
mindful of hardship.

2
Silence again. Silence in Spruce Tree Lodge,
at Hovenweep, Chaco Canyon,
stone and sunlight resting against each other
and no ghosts coming to converse
at nightfall when the stars spring out
and we stand on the rimrock, staring up
at the Bear and the hunters chasing him,
at the stocky women, grinding corn
among dogs, turkeys, children,
while smoke floats from the kiva
and snow-fluff crowns the sagebrush.

Silence, solstice to equinox.
Empty granaries, cold firepits, dry cisterns.
The sun walks through the canyon,
peering under the sandstone overhangs,
and the wind walks too, wearing pine-smell.
Skull-jar and serviceberry,
sipapu and alcove,
a ghostly sea of buffalo
tossing on the plains below.

And the light slips off
among the rifted mesas,
the dead are wrapped in turkey-feather blankets,
rabbit-fur robes, yucca mats,
and buried in the trashpiles,
while the living move south or west
in search of food and water
leaving it all to the sun and wind and stars
who lived here first.

The night is dreamless,
a star chart, a crescent wrench moon,
and the air hangs quietly
a sea whose bottom you walk
looking up through the empty miles,
the rocks around you like turned backs.

The sun cracks earth, the frost splits rocks.
What's history if it falls away,
if the brick-colored woman
milling corn in the courtyard
isn't kin to us, can't leave us this landscape,
neighbor horizon and brother canyon wren,
toehold and rampart,
the old river of belief
that pounds through empty gullies
like sunlight and moonlight
leaving them undisturbed?

Touch me. Moisten my mouth,
dazzle my eyes. Link me a moment to the life
that wore on gently here
and left these ruins to the sun.

3
In the swept museum,
smaller than hummingbirds
these people kneel and climb in little models
weaving their tiny baskets
hoarding their dollhouse ears of corn.

And who doesn't crouch below some diorama
while sunlight moves across a mesa,
hearing the call of raven,
glimpsing the Steller's jay?

I write this on an overhang, a porch,
against a California canyon
that runs down to the sea;
across the way the houses perch and nestle
among the live oaks, palms and avocado trees.
Hummingbirds float through my eucalyptus
like strange little fingers, or gods,
and the raven's shadow travels the rough slope,
wrinkling and stretching,
recollection of another life.

The hummingbird comes to rest, midair,
and the mind meshes with other minds,
lost patterns of thought that hang
over the mesas, across the hillsides,
in pools of light and shadow,
and make us bow in thought or prayer,
silence or speech,
while the sun that walked this canyon
when it was brown and empty
and will have it so again
carries the day away
through dry and shining air.

Laguna Beach. September 1981

October Couplets

1

Again the cold: shot bolt, blue shackle,
oxalic acid bleaching a rubber cuff,

a cow-eyed giantess burning roots and brush,
the streak and smash of clouds, loud settling jays,

crows roosting closer—my older-by-one-year bones
have their own dull hum, a blues: it's all plod,

but they want to go on, above timberline,
to boulders, florets, ozone, then go free

in the old mill that the wind and the frost run
all day all night under the gauze and gaze of stars.

2

Somewhere between sperm cell and clam shell
this space cruiser takes me places I'd rather

stay clear of: a planet all graveyard, mowed,
graveled and paved, bride-light and parson-shade,

or a milkweed, bitter, about to burst, or a dropped
acorn even a squirrel didn't want, browning to black,

and I have to learn to relax with it all, to sing
"Where the bee sucks, there suck I," though the lily

is sticky and choking, bees don't suck, and the sting
is a greeting you never recover from.

3

"Steam of consciousness," a student's fluke,
makes me see a lake, linen-white at evening,

some amnesia-happy poet all curled up
sucking a rock at its black bottom;

oblivion tempts everyone, but I
would miss too much—whales and ticks,

the weather's subtle bustle, blue crab clouds,
my kite rising, paper and sticks, a silver ember,

while the poem's ghost waits by the empty band shell,
does a little tango, taps out its own last line.

4

But this fall rain, somehow both thread and button,
sewing itself to the malachite grass,

beading the clubs and brushes of the spruce—
all day I have sat as if gazing over water,

wind feathering the reservoir, stupid as a church,
and thought of summer: all those burst horizons,

mineral cities, rosy meat, clean seas and shaggy islands,
the wine cork popping in the grape arbor,

these things seem better and clearer than gods just
    now,
raspberries hung like lamps among their brambles.

5

These leaves, these paper cutouts drifting the yard,
stars, fish, mittens, saddles: the badges and epaulets

of emptiness—last night in my dream
I was the killer, the guard who failed to stop him,

and the child who froze and was spared: Nothing
    lasts,
sang the crowd, and I answered, It sure does;

Is nothing sacred, roared the statesman—I do
believe it is, said I . . . I wake and shave,

still full of my dreamflood—oh skim milk sky,
oh brown star curling in my hand . . .

Bashō

Tonight, on the other side of the lake,
someone is walking with a lantern.

The changing light on the water
—a blossom, a wasp, a blowfish—
calls me back from desolation
and makes me sigh with pleasure.

How can I be so foolish?

*

It's true! All night
I listen to the rain
dripping in a basin . . .
in the morning I have a haiku.
So what!

All these years
and I think I know
just about nothing:
a close-grained man
standing in haze by the warm lake
hearing the slap of oars
and sobbing.

*

For weeks now, months, a year,
I have been living here at Unreal Hut
trying to decide what delight means
and what to do with my loneliness.

Wearing a black robe,
weaving around like a bat . . .

    *

Fallen persimmon, shriveled chestnut,
I see myself too clearly.

A poet named for a banana tree!

Some lines of my own come back:
Year after year
on the monkey's face—
a monkey mask.

I suppose I know what I want:
the calm of a wooden Buddha,
the state of mind of that monk
who forgot about the snow
even as he was sweeping it!

But I can't turn away from the world.
I sit and stare for hours at
a broken pot or a bruised peach.
An owl's call makes me dance.

I remember a renga we wrote
that had some lines by Boncho:
somebody dusts the ashes
from a grilled sardine . . .
And that's the poem! That sardine!
And when it is, I feel
it is the whole world too.

But what does it mean
and how can it save you?
When my hut burned down
I stood there thinking,
"Homeless, we're all of us homeless . . ."

Or all my travels, just so much
slogging around in the mire,
and all those haiku,
squiggles of light in the water . . .

     *

Poems change nothing, save nothing.

Should the pupil love
the blows of the teacher?

A storm is passing over.
Lightning, reflected in the lake,
scares me and leaves me speechless.

I can't turn away from the world
but I can go lightly . . .

Along the way small things
may still distract me:
a crescent moon, a farmer
digging for wild potatoes,
red pepper pods, a snapped chrysanthemum . . .

Love the teacher, hate the blows.

Standing in mist by the shore,
nothing much on my mind . . .

*

Wearing a black robe,
weaving around like a bat—
or crossing a wide field
wearing a cypress hat!

Six Ghosts

The Suicide

You think I opened this door
on an impulse. I wish that were true.
But the door was there all my life.
Even when I looked away
I could feel its cold outline.
It knew. Knew I would touch the strange handle,
take one last breath, swing it ajar,
enter that room
empty of me.

The Hunter

The deer that had bedded down
in the second growth by the creek
started up and was gone
before my eyes and ears
could take it in.

Now, among mind-shaped trees,
I run ahead of the deer when I want to.

The Sailor

If I come back to the moment of my death,
the ship coasting across black water
its sails half-furled, glowing white
and the storm looming beyond—

If I come back it is not regret
but because I am part of some huge dance
that takes me there, breathless and laughing.

The Simpleton

Soap and the moon and my crown askew.

The Poet

All of the words cracked open
and I hatched out
to the world I used to watch
from the distance of my head:
thunder-scrubbed rainbows,
ploughed fields like rosy cocoa-dust,
and that voice, echoing behind me.

The Reader

Now that my life is a cool book
I have read once, I can come back
to browse. Often I turn
to a chapter where nothing happened.
Even that is unbearably full,
and I stare at a single page for days,
its strange marks, its wild white silence.

The Self: A Sonnet Sequence

1

If we are what we see, hear, handle,
then I am London now: rainlight and chimneypots,
shuddering buses, streaky bacon flatblocks,
rooks in a queue. Reading your novel, I was a girl

who took up living in a barn. Sense-pestered,
trailing itself around the world,
the self is now and then complete as it looks in
to mingle with an afternoon, a page, a person . . .

In the Siberian frozen tombs they found
wool socks, expressive faces, rugs, fresh leather,
a chieftain's arm still glowing with tattoos:

what the self freezes, what the self digs up—
what do you want to call it, kid?
Weather. A city on a page. A mirror.

2

Self as imperialist, pushing out his borders?
Oh, the ego rides in armor, bellows threats,
but his helmet's a pocked kettle, he'll turn tail
as soon as he sees the torches of the future,

he's far less real than, say, his horse's shoulder.
The anarchists he hired are dismantling
what's left of his soft palace, heaving chunks
into the soft and unbecoming river.

A candle: what it means to do is vanish,
brightly. The self: what it means to do
is make a candle. Something of that kind,

and the object—horseshoe, cabbage, poem—
is what the self just hoped to run together to
and fill: a cup of anonymity.

3
Well, no, not run together. Scatter: smoke
in its eloquent hoods and cowls. Clouds,
their race and rain. We're swarms of funny matter
(ice, rust, grasses, moonsparks, puff-paste)

longing and fearing to disperse. "Can't get away
from you-know-who" (scratched on a mirror), but
    the eye
sees way beyond the eye, and the mooncalf mind
sits on its shelf and flies great kites.

"After the dancers have left
and the grand ballroom is empty,
the old beekeeper brings

a rustling and humming box;
and the band begins to play again,
but you've never heard the music."

4

My young self comes to see me, fresh and friendly.
He is from 1957, and anxious to get back.
I think he is just polite about my acting
as though we had lots in common. Stands in
   the doorway,

charming but rushed. I'm amazed
that I like him so much, like him at *all,*
he has such an air of self-discovery,
as if one day to the next he *knows* himself

(first love, acting, superficial poems),
a life he thinks I'm merely interrupting.
I live inside his dream, he inside mine,

and we back away from each other, smiling,
a couple of meadows, a couple of knives,
affection brimming between us as we go.

5

Is a pebble. Is a bubble. Drags its little sled
through empty salt flats under a cobalt sky
of nailed-up stars. Is a lamb with real sharp teeth,
a tongue waltzing in a moonlit clearing. Is

a donkey, leaning against a mulberry tree
in which the silkworms spin their mysteries;
hugs itself, hugs itself and cries,
a horn full of sparks, a shadow at a keyhole.

The critic wanted to enter the very brush stroke,
then find the brush, then climb the painter's arm,
muscle and vein and nerve to mind and heart:

instead he stumbled and then he was falling forever
through meaningless words that were falling too
in exactly the opposite direction.

6
Has its parents strapped on like backpacks,
grandparents in a suitcase; its orders are
to move the grand piano over a mountain
without upsetting the buckets of milk for its children.

The house is sheared open by the wrecking ball
and there is the bathroom, flashing its mirror,
the wallpaper, losing track of its pattern,
the chest of drawers where father kept his condoms.

Tear rolling down the hill of the corpse's
cheek. Big tear that rolls off the stiff blue chin.
Things left behind, trashbin and junkyard.

Rain won't be different from skin.
Eye won't be different from view.
Smoke will take root and every flower float.

7

Hyde, this is Jekyll: no more rages,
no more rapes and stranglings. I leave this flat
only for necessary shopping.
On the horizon, the orphanage burns.

Evelyn Waugh, timid of ridicule,
built up a carapace so thick
he could hardly move inside it—except to write
painful, hilarious novels, ridiculing the world.

The daylight brightens, dims and brightens.
Late March. Atoms of nostalgia,
flakes of essential self. Crusoe on his beach

pondering a footprint. Still March. Outside
the blown rain writes nonsense on the windows,
the pear tree strains against its ivory buds.

8

One of those houses where the eyes of portraits move
and suits of armor mutter by the stairs.
But this was worse. The chairs had body-heat
and every sink was specked with blood.

I swept from room to room, my cape
billowing out behind. Sat by the fire
poking the panting coals. Hid beneath a bed
and listened to them screwing in the attic.

Think of a liquid. Dog slobber. Cattle drool.
Dipped up in a leaf-cup from a spring. It's true,
anything other than human could comfort me now

like that French poet who could put his face
against a hanging side of beef
and still his fear.

9
Good-bye to the night sky, the Milky Way
a bone-seam on a cranium, vein in a cave.
Now dawn is a rooster, noon a pheasant
crossing the road. I drive. Land's End, Tintagel,

the landscape fills me slowly, like a sail.
A daylight display, a wind off the Atlantic,
ego shadows sailing across pieced fields,
a herd of clouds without a shepherd.

Sometimes the world will fit you like a sweater
and you think ingenuity and fortitude
can see you through, your recipe and axis.

I have to say this clumsily; at best,
the image trembles in its instant, star
in a pail of water carried through a glade.

10

In Voronezh did Mandelstam
sing of his death the winter I was born
in Davenport, in Iowa, all mother's milk and love
against his sour tea and fear. The contrast

makes me wince. I want . . . to be a goldfinch too?
No, and I'm not the point. Nor Mandelstam. We're
    both
exhibits of the self, the flesh made word,
singing its own confusion and delight:

all this takes place despite the big world's Stalins.
I write this in the Royal Mail, in Islington.
"Hullo, Stanley," says the barmaid. Pool balls click,

the jukebox throbs. We bob on currents,
taking the world as best we can, each planet
cruising its dawns and dusks around the sun.

England. January-May 1979

3

Hunting for Mushrooms in Orange County

Like a snail on a cabbage leaf
I move along this hillside.

Blank eyeballs bulging in the grass,
doorknobs to darkness, night's white knuckles,
the scattered cups and saucers of the dead,
old smoky hard-ons coaxed up by the rain!

There are stars and flowers in this world,
green sprouts, plump nuts, threshed grain,
fruit in bright rinds and clusters—

but there are these buttons too,
these pallid lamps, lit by a secret,
tokens so strange we hold our breath to eat them,
puffball, campestris, morel,
wrinkled and chalky blebs of foam.

I look up from my gathering
and think I don't know where I am . . .
the buckskin hills, the instant cities,
this grainy earth we find and lose
and find again
and learn to say we shall lie down in,

meanwhile nibbling on these swollen caps
beautiful messages of decay, from roots, bones, teeth,
from coal and bark, humus and pulp and sperm,
muzzle-skull, channel and hand, the all-containing
    dead,

invisible branchings of our living smolder—
I glance around me, half-bewildered,
here in this California sunlight
spore dust drifting right through my body

a meadow-mushroom humming between my fingers.

Suite for Jean Follain

1

In September there come to Ohio
clouds out of old Dutch paintings
above weeds in gold confusion
in overlooked orchards apples
drop in the wild grass
a baby strapped in a station wagon
stares at the checked jackets
of hunters stooping to gather
groceries spilled on the sidewalk.

2

Never came back to visit
says the old woman out loud
lugging a bucket of feed
across the empty farmyard
beyond her a shed is collapsing
terrifically slowly a cow
is chewing without expression
white stars pass
from a burst milkweed.

3

The evening has turned the blue
of a milk of magnesia bottle
and the big American flag
is snapping against itself
in front of the courthouse
looking up at the window
where she undressed he thinks
of wrens and tent revivals
and statues from ancient Egypt.

4

A wet stone beehive
stands in the middle of the garden
beyond the wall delivery trucks
occasionally pass
a smell of burning leaves
reminds the mailman of childhood
a fish jumps in the reservoir
in the graveyard clumps of honey mushrooms
blacken slowly in rain.

Elegy in the Form of an Invitation

James Wright, b. 1927, Martin's Ferry, Ohio;
d. 1980, New York City

Early spring in Ohio. Lines
of thunderstorms, quiet flares
on the southern horizon.
A doctor stares at his hands.
His friend the schoolmaster
plays helplessly with a thread.

I know you have put your voice aside
and entered something else.

I like to think you could come back here now
like a man returning to his body
after a long dream of pain and terror.

It wouldn't all be easy:
sometimes the wind blows birds
right off their wires and branches,
chemical wastes smolder on weedy sidings,
codgers and crones still starve in shacks
in the hills above Portsmouth and Welfare . . .
hobo, cathouse, slagheap, old mines
that never exhaust their veins—
it is all the way you said.

But there is this fierce green
and bean shoots poking through potting soil
and in a month or so the bees
will move like sparks among the roses.

And I like to think
the things that hurt won't hurt you any more
and that you will come back
in the spring, for the quiet,
the dark shine of grackles,
raccoon tracks by the river,
the moon's ghost in the afternoon,
and the black earth behind the plowing.

Vermont Summer:
Three Snapshots, One Letter

Imaginary Polaroid

In this picture I am standing in a meadow,
holding a list of fifty-one wildflowers.
It is Vermont, midsummer, clear morning
all the way to the Adirondacks.
I am, as usual, lost. But happy,
shaggy with dew. Waving my list.
The wind that blows the clouds across these mountains
has blown my ghosts away, and the sun
has flooded my world to the blinding-point.
There's nothing to do till galaxy-rise
but name and gather the wildflowers.
This is called "pearly everlasting."
And this one is arrow-leaved tear-thumb!
Hawkweed, stitchwort, dogbane, meadow-rue . . .
The dark comes on, the fireflies weave around me,
pearl and phosphor in the windy dark,
and still I am clutching my list,
saying "hop clover, fireweed, cinquefoil,"
as the Milky Way spreads like an anchor overhead.

Robert Frost's Cabin

He perched up here at the lip of the woods
summer after summer. Grafted his apple trees
into a state of confusion. Came down
two or three times a season to be lionized.
Mesmerized visitors with talk,
or hid from them. Or both.

Charles and I look in his windows.
There's the famous chair.
The place is tiny, but the view is good.
We shake our heads at his solitude.
Couldn't he have the kind of friendship
that brought us up here together?

How can we keep from becoming such molluscs?
Easy, says Charles: Don't live that long.

Hay-Henge

After the meadow was mowed and before
the bales were gathered, the students
erected a midget Stonehenge in the moonlight.
It stood there all the next day:
real from a distance, and up close
sweet-smelling and short-lived.

Off and on I've been pondering models:
I think they are all we have.
Snapshots, cabins, lists. Metonymies.
At Lascaux they've opened
a replica of the caves. I shall get
Peter Quince to write a ballad of this dream . . .
The sun goes down beyond Hay-Henge;
clouds and mountains mix in the distance.

Letter to Chloe

Since you left, we've had
wild blackberries, northern lights,
and one grand thunderstorm.
Again, these mountains have been
Chinese with their graduated mist.
Tonight it's clear and we hope to see
a meteor shower. I'm teaching Vaughan,
who tried to show us another world
with images of light, and knew
he needed dark to make the light more real.

I shake my head, still lost.
I'm lucky if I find a berry,
name a flower, see a shooting star.
You and I cried a little at the airport:
each parting's a model for something bigger.
But I don't think the models mean much.
We try to take them as they come:
a trefoil in the hand, a meteor trail
crossing the retina, a black and glinting
tart-sweet berry in the mouth.

Bonuses

The wasp's
zigzag journey
up the window
while I read
down one
page.

    *

Mushrooms as ghosts:
did you think rot
could fruit this way?
Or taste like this?
Or give you visions?

    *

The grackle walks
like a drum major
then leaps straight up
and opens,
a lady's fan.

    *

Mushroom architecture:
Art Deco airport towers,
Destroying Angels pure as mosques,
geodesic puffballs, shagged pagodas,
morels by Gaudi . . .

    *

Because of the way
the windows join
their images I see
two robins now—
one solid on the lawn,
the other, next to him,
a see-through ghost.

The solitary double, fierce for worms,
struts unaware of what's not there.

Three Walks

Near "Appleby," Axminster, Devon. June 1982

A path, a garden, a country lane
with a very old lady and her daughter,
the whole evening holding tremulous
as though it might never end.
A codger watering his broccoli
talks up the art of gardening as
we gaze at his cabbages and gooseberries.
By his garden wall and along the lane
foxglove is speechlessly in bloom,
herb Robert, hogweed, eglantine,
everything, even the grass and cuckoo-spittle,
touched with the slow welling-up of life.
When we come back I hear again
some thrush in the deep shade
making a music as intricate
as what we were walking through.

Near Arcidosso, Tuscany. July 1979

Maybe I like this city for being
nearly unknown, off in the mountains.
Over and over the cuckoo calls from the chestnuts
this sleepy midday. Red and lemon posters
for a circus, ORFEI, plaster every wall,
and I can imagine a humdrum Orpheus
ambling the narrow street to the bakery,
pausing to stare
at the round fountain where a stone mask
blows a thin rope of water
into a basin, a rope without ends.
He would climb to the old castle,
baking in sunshine, where
the air is alive with bees

that build in the crumbling masonry.
What would he make of it all? Would he stand,
his eyes blurring with tears
looking back through the smoke of time
at the men and women, come and gone,
who have seen how the earth is lovely
and seen how it meanings desert them?

Near Lorain and Oberlin, Ohio. July 1982

Backward and forward in time, as if
by way of England and Italy, I've come
to stand in the K-Mart parking lot
while Cassiopeia hangs askew
beyond the cornfields, come to hear doves
calling all morning in the rain
like very tired cuckoos.
Tomorrow, the Fourth of July, I'll go
mushroom-gathering in the cemetery
to the rumble of summer thunder
among the distant dead, Huron Weed, Amanda
    Peabody,
and the newer dead I knew, George Lanyi, Jean Tufts,
and if it's not so time-caressed
still I will pause there, startled,
as though I stood on my own heart
in nature's haunted house,
as again, in the long-drawn evening,
with the fireflies signaling: J, J, J,
and the skyrockets in the distance:
foxgloves, fountains, bees,
constellations and mushrooms,
hung for a second or two
on the dim sky above the trees.

Notes and Dedications

The Emily Dickinson poem quoted as epigraph is Number 1400 in the *Complete Poems*. Its conjectured date is 1877.

"In My Own Back Yard" is for Warren and Judy Sheldon.

"Two Trips to Ireland" is for Andrew and Marjorie Hoover.

"Mesa Verde" contains two words that may be unfamiliar to many readers. "Anasazi" is a Pueblo word meaning "the old people" or "the ancients," i.e., the builders of Mesa Verde and other ruins in the area. "Sipapu" means "soul-hole," from which human beings were supposed to have first emerged.

"October Couplets" is for Richard Kent.

Much of my information about Bashō is drawn from Makoto Ueda, *Matsuo Bashō* (Kodansha, 1982).

For one comparison in "Six Ghosts" I am indebted to the journals of Gerard Manley Hopkins.

The "you" in the first sonnet is Reina Calderon, a student, and the italicized line is from a poem she wrote for a workshop I taught.

"Hunting for Mushrooms in Orange County" is for Charles and Holly Wright.

"Suite for Jean Follain" is for Keith Hollaman.

"Three Walks" is for David Walker.

I would like to thank the Guggenheim Foundation and the National Endowment for the Arts for grants that supported the writing of this book.

About the Author

David Young is professor of English at Oberlin College; co-editor of the literary magazine *Field*, and arbiter of *Field*'s translation series; translator of Chinese, German, and Czechoslovakian poetry; an established Shakespearean scholar; and a birdwatcher and mushroom hunter. A graduate of Carleton College (B.A., 1958), he earned a Ph.D. from Yale University (1965). He received a Guggenheim fellowship in 1979 and is the author of four collections of poems. He lives in Oberlin, Ohio.

About the Book

This book has been composed in Garamond #3 by Compositors of Cedar Rapids, Iowa. It has been printed on 60 pound Sebago by Kingsport Press of Kingsport, Tennessee. It has been bound by Kingsport Press of Kingsport, Tennessee. Dust jackets and covers have been printed by Phoenix Color Corporation of Long Island City, New York.

Other books by David Young

Poems

Sweating Out the Winter

Boxcars

Work Lights: Thirty-two Prose Poems

The Names of a Hare in English

Translations

Rilke, *Duino Elegies*

Four T'ang Poets

Valuable Nail: Selected Poems of Gunter Eich
   (*with Stuart Friebert and David Walker*)

Miroslav Holub, *Interferon, or On Theater*
   (*with Dana Hábová*)

Criticism

Something of Great Constancy: The Art of
   "A Midsummer Night's Dream"
The Heart's Forest: Shakespeare's
   Pastoral Plays

Anthologies

Twentieth Century Interpretations of "2 Henry IV"

A FIELD Guide to Contemporary Poetry and Poetics
   (*with Stuart Friebert*)

The Longman Anthology of Contemporary American
   Poetry
   (*with Stuart Friebert*)

Magical Realist Fiction (*with Keith Hollaman*)